Fact Finders

LAND and WATER

Lake Superior

by Anne Ylvisaker

Consultant:
Rosanne W. Fortner, Professor of Natural Resources
and Associate Director, F. T. Stone Laboratory
The Ohio State University
School of Natural Resources
Columbus, Ohio

Capstone *press*

Mankato, Minnesota

Fact Finders is published by Capstone Press
151 Good Counsel Drive, P.O. Box 669, Mankato, Minnesota 56002
http://www.capstone-press.com

Library of Congress Cataloging-in-Publication Data
Ylvisaker, Anne.
    Lake Superior / by Anne Ylvisaker.
    p. cm.—(Fact finders. Land and water)
    Summary: A brief introduction to the largest of North America's Great Lakes,
discussing Lake Superior's creation, early history, shipping industry, and its importance
today.
    Includes bibliographical references and index.
    ISBN 0-7368-2212-7 (hardcover)
    1. Superior, Lake—Juvenile literature. [1. Superior, Lake.] I. Title. II. Series.
F552.Y58 2004
977.4'9—dc21   2003001668

Editorial Credits
Erika L. Shores, editor; Juliette Peters, designer and illustrator; Alta Schaffer,
    photo researcher; Eric Kudalis, product planning editor

Photo Credits
Cover image: Shores of Lake Superior, PhotoDisc, Inc./Scenics of America/PhotoLink

Corbis/Charles E. Rotkin, 5
Doranne Jacobson, 11
Timepix/George Skadding, 21; Andrew Sacks, 22
James P. Rowan, 1
Kay Shaw, 25
North Wind Picture Archives, 16–17, 19
Stock Montage Inc., 12–13, 15
Richard Hamilton Smith, 27
Root Resources/Bill Glass, 10; Jana R. Jirak, 26
Visualizing the Great Lakes - Images of a Region, 23

The Hands On activity on page 29 was adapted with permission from "How Big Is a Crowd?"
by R. W. Fortner and D. Jax, LAKERS Observe Coastweeks, Columbus, Ohio: Sea Grant
Education Program.

1 2 3 4 5 6 08 07 06 05 04 03

Table of Contents

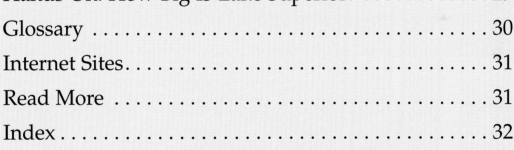

Chapter 1

Lake Superior

November brings the worst storms on Lake Superior. On November 10, 1975, Captain Ernest McSorley got ready for a storm coming from the southwest.

Captain McSorley was the captain of one of the largest ships on the Great Lakes. The *Edmund Fitzgerald* was 729 feet (222 meters) long and weighed more than 13,000 tons (11,800 metric tons). It carried iron ore and sometimes people.

Big waves soon washed over the ship's deck. Winds blew at 90 miles (145 kilometers) per hour. Captain McSorley talked by radio with another ship. "We are holding our own," he said. Seconds later, his ship disappeared.

The *Edmund Fitzgerald* carried iron ore to ports on the Great Lakes.

The *Edmund Fitzgerald* was found in two pieces at the bottom of Lake Superior. One part is right side up and the other upside down. No one knows for sure why the ship sank. All 29 crew members died.

The Great Lakes

The Great Lakes of North America are Lake Superior, Lake Huron, Lake Michigan, Lake Erie, and Lake Ontario. Straits and rivers join the Great Lakes to each other and to the Atlantic Ocean. Together, rivers, canals, and lakes make up the St. Lawrence Seaway. The seaway is a path to ship goods from the Atlantic Ocean to ports on the Great Lakes.

Lake Superior is the largest and deepest of the Great Lakes. One-tenth of the world's fresh water is in Lake Superior.

Lake Superior is also the cleanest, clearest, and coldest Great Lake. The average water temperature is 40 degrees Fahrenheit (4.4 degrees Celsius).

Lake Superior is the largest Great Lake.

Shores of Lake Superior

The shores around Lake Superior are varied. Forests cover Lake Superior's rocky north shore. The southern shores of Lake Superior have sandstone cliffs and pebble beaches.

Chapter 2

Lake Beginnings

Long ago, volcanos covered the Lake Superior area. The rocky areas along Lake Superior's north shore may be what is left of those volcanos.

After thousands of years, Earth grew cold. Sheets of ice covered the Great Lakes area. These glaciers were more than 1 mile (2 kilometers) thick and pressed down on the ground. Glaciers also moved rocks that scraped the ground. The pressure and scraping carved wide valleys. When the glaciers melted, their water filled the valleys. This made the Great Lakes.

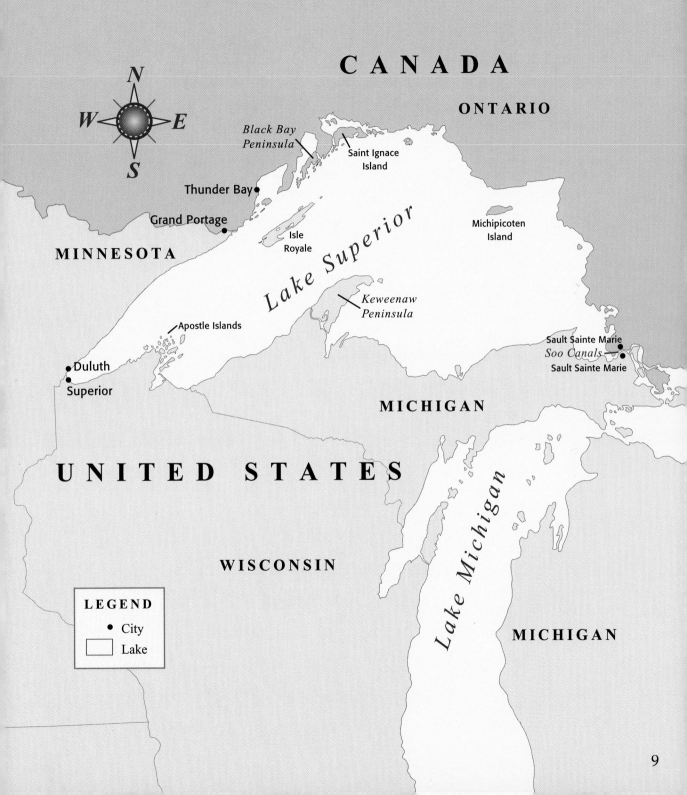

CANADA

ONTARIO

Black Bay
Peninsula

Saint Ignace
Island

Thunder Bay •

Grand Portage •

MINNESOTA

Isle
Royale

Lake Superior

Michipicoten
Island

Keweenaw
Peninsula

Apostle Islands

Sault Sainte Marie
Soo Canals
Sault Sainte Marie

• Duluth

• Superior

MICHIGAN

UNITED STATES

Lake Michigan

WISCONSIN

MICHIGAN

LEGEND

• City

☐ Lake

Peninsulas and Islands

Glaciers formed peninsulas and islands. Today,
two long peninsulas, Keweenaw and Black Bay
Peninsulas, stretch into Lake Superior. Several
large islands also dot the lake. Isle Royale is Lake
Superior's largest island. Other islands include the
Apostle Islands, Saint Ignace, and Michipicoten.

The Soo Canals

The St. Marys River joins Lake Superior and Lake Huron. Rapids on the river make it impossible for boats to travel between the two lakes. The Soo Canals were built so boats could go around the rapids.

Chapter 3

Early People

Some of the earliest people living around Lake Superior were Old Copper Indians. Between 3,000 and 7,000 years ago, these people used copper to make tools, utensils, and fishing hooks. They hunted and fished.

By A.D. 1600, Ojibwa Indians lived around Lake Superior. In summer, groups of Ojibwa gathered by the lake to fish. They used hooks, spears, and nets. In late summer, they gathered berries and wild rice. In fall, the Ojibwa spread out over the area to hunt for moose, beaver, bear, and other animals. They hunted with spears, bows and arrows, and traps.

Ojibwa Indians lived near Lake Superior.

Early Explorers

In 1622, Étienne Brulé was the first European to come to Lake Superior. He returned 37 years later with French fur trappers and traders. At that time in Europe, fur coats and hats were popular.

Voyageurs

Voyageurs were men who explored the Great Lakes area and brought back animal furs. Voyageurs often paddled their canoes all day. They stopped only to have a small meal and rest. They knew the Indian tribes and traded with them for furs. The Indians traded furs for weapons and cooking pots.

Voyageurs and American Indians met to trade furs and other goods.

Rendezvous

A rendezvous (RON-deh-voo) was held each July. This gathering brought together about 3,000 voyageurs and Indians. They met for two weeks of trading. Voyageurs brought their furs to Grand Portage. Some traveled more than 1,800 miles (2,900 kilometers) to the rendezvous.

Chapter 4

Industry

More people came to the areas around
Lake Superior in the 1800s. The
American Fur Company set up fishing
camps near the lake. Fishermen sold

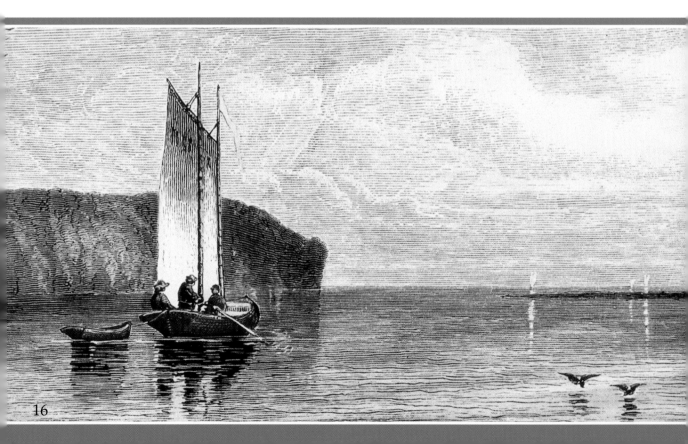

what they caught to the company.
Fishermen sometimes caught whitefish
and trout to sell in nearby villages.

By the mid-1800s, people began to
mine around Lake Superior. They mined
copper and iron. The miners and their
families built towns around the lake.

Fishermen used nets to catch fish in Lake Superior.

With fur, fish, and minerals to move, shipping became more important. The Soo Canals opened in 1855. Passenger ships also started traveling on the lake because more people were living there.

By the late 1800s, logging was a booming business in the towns near Lake Superior. Loggers cut down trees. They rolled the cut trees into the rivers to float to sawmills. Lake Superior's northern forests were almost cut bare in a period called The Big Cut.

The Big Cut

White pine trees were cut down in North America between 1776 and 1940. The trees were used to build 52 million homes, 12 million farm houses, 2 million schools and libraries, 650 churches, and 450,000 factories.

Chapter 5

Problems

In the 1930s, sea lampreys entered the Great Lakes from the Atlantic Ocean. These jawless creatures suck the blood and other body fluids from fish such as trout and salmon. Many fish died. The lack of fish hurt the fishing industry.

In the 1970s, scientists stopped the lampreys from entering the lakes. Fish were added to the lake. The return of fish to the lake helped the fishing industry.

Zebra mussels are another threat to the health of Lake Superior. These tiny shellfish live in other areas of the world. They attach themselves to ships that sail

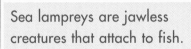

Sea lampreys are jawless
creatures that attach to fish.

into the Great Lakes. Many zebra mussels are carried in the water stored in the bottom of large ships. The zebra mussels eat the algae that are food for fish. Without the algae, fish starve. Scientists are working to control the zebra mussels. Inspectors check ships for the mussels before the ships enter ports on Lake Superior and the other Great Lakes.

Zebra mussels attach themselves to a hard surface to survive.

Pollution

Long ago, people thought Lake Superior was so big it could handle anything. People dumped waste into the lake. Chemicals from farms and factories washed into rivers and then into the lake. In 1972, U.S. and Canadian officials signed the Great Lakes Water Quality Agreement. People living around the Great Lakes agreed to work together to keep the lakes healthy.

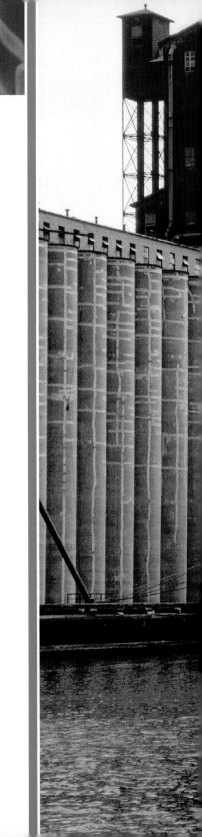

Chapter 6

Lake Superior Today

Today, Lake Superior is a busy place for industry and shipping. Logging continues to be an important industry around Lake Superior. Trees are made into lumber and paper.

Duluth, Minnesota, and Thunder Bay, Ontario, are among the busiest shipping ports in the world. Goods such as grain and iron ore are shipped around the world from these ports.

Tourism is important to the towns around the lake. People come from all over the world to enjoy the natural beauty of the area. Some people go

Ships such as this one carry grain and other cargo.

camping, canoeing, and kayaking in the quiet wilderness. Others hunt and fish. Shipwatching is a popular activity in Duluth. Scuba divers come to view the shipwrecks that still lie at the bottom of the lake.

Lake Superior is important to the people living around it. People work to keep Lake Superior and its nearby areas clean and healthy.

Kayaking is a popular activity on Lake Superior.

People can view ships entering the port at Duluth, Minnesota.

Fast Facts

Length: 350 miles (563 kilometers)

Width: 160 miles (257 kilometers)

Average depth: 489 feet (149 meters)

Maximum depth: 1,333 feet (406 meters)

Shoreline length: 2,730 miles (4,393 kilometers)

Population surrounding the lake: 673,000

Name: French explorers first called Lake Superior "le lac superieur." This means "upper lake" in French.

Fish: More than 60 kinds of fish live in Lake Superior. Some of these fish are brook trout, lake sturgeon, lake whitefish, northern pike, and walleye.

Hands On: *How Big Is Lake Superior?*

Lake Superior is the largest Great Lake. You can see how big it is compared to the other four lakes by trying this activity.

What You Need

Measuring tape
String
A large open area
Masking tape

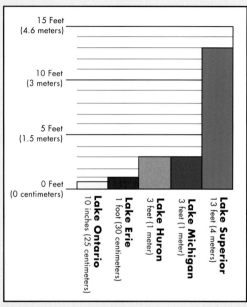

What You Do

1. Measure one piece of string 13 feet (4 meters) long. This string will stand for Lake Superior.
2. Measure four more pieces of string for the other four lakes. Use the chart shown above.
3. Make a loop out of each string. Tie the ends together. You will have five loops of string.
4. Using the map on page 7, tape the loops to the ground to show the Great Lakes. The smallest loop is Lake Ontario. The largest loop is Lake Superior.
5. Pick up the loop that is Lake Ontario. Can you place it inside the Lake Superior loop? Does the loop of Lake Erie fit inside Lake Superior as well? Can you imagine how much bigger Lake Superior really is compared to the other Great Lakes?

Glossary

canal (kun-NAL)—a channel that is dug across land; canals join bodies of water so that ships can travel between them.

glacier (GLAY-shur)—a large, slow-moving sheet of ice and snow

industry (IN-duh-stree)—businesses that make products or provide services

mine (MINE)—to dig up minerals that are underground

peninsula (puh-NIN-suh-luh)—land that is surrounded by water on three sides

port (PORT)—a place where boats and ships can dock safely

region (REE-juhn)—a large area of land or water

Internet Sites

Do you want to find out more about Lake Superior?
Let FactHound, our fact-finding hound dog, do the
research for you.

Here's how:
1) Visit *http://www.facthound.com*
2) Type in the **BOOK ID** number: **0736822127**
3) Click on **FETCH IT**.

FactHound will fetch Internet sites picked by our editors just for you!

Read More

Prevost, John F. *Lake Superior.* Rivers and Lakes. Edina, Minn.:
Abdo, 2002.

Todd, Anne M. *The Ojibwa: People of the Great Lakes.* American
Indian Nations. Mankato, Minn.: Bridgestone Books, 2003.

Index